HÄGAR
THE HORRIBLE #2

BY DIK BROWNE

tempo
books
GROSSET & DUNLAP
A Filmways Company
Publishers • New York

Meet Hägar the Horrible, a typical, hard-working, barbarian businessman (sacking and looting)

His wife Helga

Their problem son Hamlet (he refuses to grow his hair to a decent length, washes almost daily, and reads books)

Their still unmarried daughter Honi (she's 16)

And Hägar's sidekick, Lucky Eddie—

Who collectively appear in close to 600 Sunday and daily papers, read by 35 million people!

THERE SHOULD BE A
LAW AGAINST MEN WITH
BEARDS DRINKING SOUP.

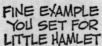

WHAT'S A DEVIL?

HE'S THE MOST EVIL, ROTTEN, DIRTY...

AND HE'S RED AND HAIRY AND HAS HORNS...

© King Features Syndicate, Inc. 1974.

6-13

AND HE...

AND HE'S ENGLISH! DID I TELL YOU THAT? HE'S ENGLISH!

OH, WORDS OF LOVE
OH, WORDS DIVINE

THE SILVER THOUGHT THE GOLDEN LINE

DIK BROWNE

OF ALL MEN'S WORDS THERE'S NONE SO FINE

© King Features Syndicate, Inc., 1974.

6-6

AS THESE THREE WORDS...
"I GOT MINE"

I GOT SOME GOOD NEWS AND SOME BAD NEWS — THE GALLEY IS ON FIRE AND WE'VE SPRUNG A LEAK.

2-26

WHAT'S THE GOOD NEWS?

ALL THE RATS HAVE LEFT THE SHIP.

© King Features Syndicate, Inc., 1974.

DIK BROWNE